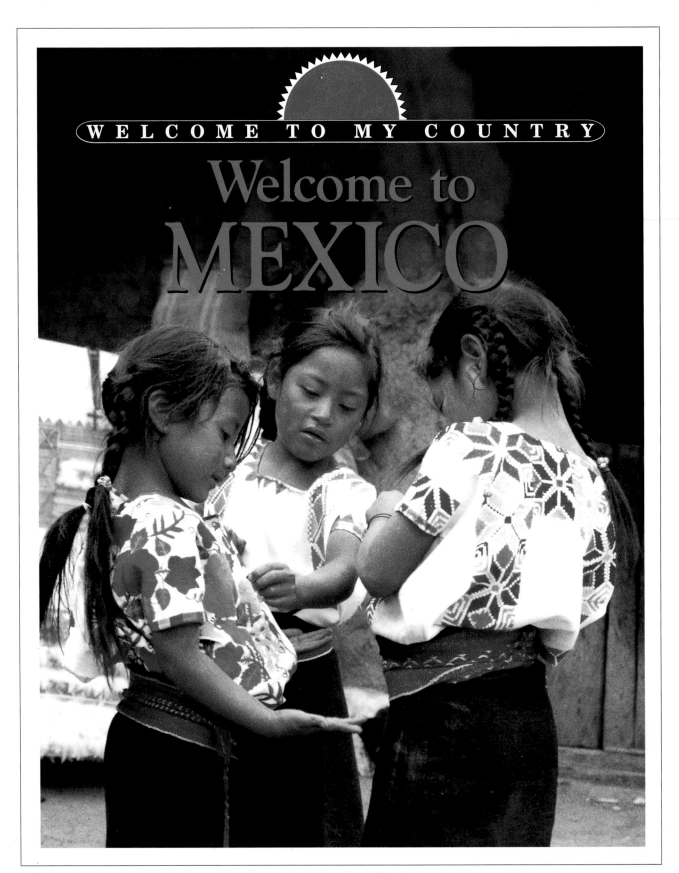

WELCOME TO MY COUNTRY

Welcome to
MEXICO

Gareth Stevens Publishing
MILWAUKEE

Written by
LESLIE JERMYN/FIONA CONBOY

Designed by
SHARIFAH FAUZIAH

Picture research by
SUSAN JANE MANUEL

First published in North America in 1999 by
Gareth Stevens Publishing
1555 North RiverCenter Drive, Suite 201
Milwaukee, Wisconsin 53212 USA

For a free color catalog describing
Gareth Stevens Publishing's list of high-quality books
and multimedia programs, call
1-800-542-2595 (USA) or
1-800-461-9120 (CANADA).
Gareth Stevens Publishing's
Fax: (414) 225-0377.

© **TIMES EDITIONS PTE LTD 1999**
Originated and designed by
Times Books International
an imprint of Times Editions Pte Ltd
Times Centre, 1 New Industrial Road
Singapore 536196
http://www.timesone.com.sg/te

Library of Congress Cataloging-in-Publication Data

Jermyn, Leslie.
Welcome to Mexico / Leslie Jermyn and Fiona Conboy.
p. cm. — (Welcome to my country)
Includes bibliographical references and index.
Summary: An overview of the history, geography, government,
economy, people, and culture of Mexico.
ISBN 0-8368-2398-2 (lib.bdg.)
1. Mexico—Juvenile literature. [1. Mexico.]
I. Conboy, Fiona. II. Title. III. Series.
F1208.5.J472   1999
972—dc21   99-22536

Printed in Malaysia

1 2 3 4 5 6 7 8 9 03 02 01 00 99

PICTURE CREDITS
A.N.A. Press Agency: 12, 22, 23 (bottom)
Andes Press Agency: 10, 20, 23 (top)
Bes Stock: 30
Focus Team: 27 (bottom)
The Hutchison Library: 1, 2, 3 (top), 7, 19,
    29, 32, 40
The Image Bank: 17
Photobank Photolibrary/Singapore: cover,
    34, 45
David Simson: 3 (center), 5, 14, 21, 27
    (top), 28 (both), 37
South American Pictures: 11, 15, 18, 35,
    36, 39
Tan Chung Lee: 13, 31, 41, 53
Liba Taylor: 3 (bottom), 4, 8, 16, 38
Topham Picturepoint: 6, 9, 26, 33
Travel Ink: 25
Trip Photographic Library: 24

Digital Scanning by Superskill Graphics Pte Ltd

Contents

5 **Welcome to Mexico!**

6 **The Land**

10 **History**

16 **Government and the Economy**

20 **People and Lifestyle**

28 **Language**

30 **Arts**

34 **Leisure**

40 **Food**

42 **Map**

44 **Quick Facts**

46 **Glossary**

47 **Books, Videos, Web Sites**

48 **Index**

Words that appear in the glossary are printed in **boldface** type the first time they occur in the text.

Welcome to Mexico!

Many years ago, Mexico was ruled by the Aztecs and the Maya. Today, Mexico's population is a mixture of Spanish and Indian **ancestry**. Let's learn about the colorful history of Mexico and its people.

Opposite: In Mexican villages, donkeys are a slow but common form of transportation.

Below: Mexicans love to perform Aztec dances at festival time.

The Flag of Mexico

The Mexican flag has green, white, and red bands. The central **crest** is an Aztec symbol of an eagle eating a snake. Their god told the Aztecs to build their capital where they found an eagle eating a snake. Today, the capital is called Mexico City.

The Land

Mexico lies at the very southern border of the United States. It is a long country shaped like a hook. The form of the land changes from north to south and east to west. It has dry deserts and tropical rain forests, volcanoes and snowcapped mountains, and swampy **lagoons** and white sandy beaches.

Below: This volcanic mountain is in southern Mexico. It is called Mt. Popocatépetl, or "smoking mountain."

The Mexican Plateau is an enormous plain stretching from the north of the country to the south. This is the most populated part of Mexico. Arid deserts occupy the north. Farther south where there is heavy rainfall, green forests come into sight. On either side of the plateau are two mountain ranges running along each coastline — the Sierra Madre Occidental to the west and the Sierra Madre Oriental to the east.

Above: The cactus is a common plant in the Mexican desert where it can survive the dry heat.

Seasons

The weather in Mexico changes from one part of the country to another. The climate is hot and dry in the south and in the northern deserts. It is much colder high in the mountains.

The rainy season runs from May to August, when it rains almost every day in the central valleys. Tropical **hurricanes** occur on both coasts every year.

Below: These monarch butterflies **migrate** to Mexico from the United States and Canada to escape the winter.

Plants and Animals

You can see many different **species** of animals in Mexico. Coatimundi live in the lowland trees, jaguars stalk the rain forests, and whales swim in the warm oceans.

Many plants can also be found in Mexico. The cactus is common because it can survive desert conditions. Some people even eat cactus plants in spite of their prickly skin!

Above: Coatimundi are members of the raccoon family. They climb trees in search of food.

History

Hundreds of years ago, Mexico was ruled by native Indian tribes. By the early 1500s, the Aztecs had become one of the most powerful tribes. As a result, many other Indians became unhappy with their **domination**. In 1519, explorer Hernán Cortés arrived from Spain and defeated the Aztecs with the help of Indians he recruited. He named Mexico *New Spain*.

Below: Montezuma, the Aztec king, went into battle with Hernán Cortés in the Aztec capital of **Tenochtitlan** (tay-NOSH-teet-lan).

Freedom for Mexico

Early in the nineteenth century, the Mexican people wanted independence from Spain. After a ten-year war, an agreement was signed, and Mexico was freed.

In 1858, **civil war** raged between the Catholic Church and the people. An Indian named Benito Juárez led the people through the war. Juárez and his followers won this civil war.

Above: Father Hidalgo started the Mexican war for independence in 1810. He was killed in battle in 1811.

The Mexican Revolution

After Juárez's death, Porfirio Díaz became president and ruled Mexico for thirty-five years. During this time, the poor got poorer, and in 1910 there was a **rebellion** by the **peasants**, led by Emiliano Zapata and Francisco "Pancho" Villa. The rebellion turned into a violent war — the Mexican Revolution — that lasted ten years and killed 1.5 million people.

Below: This wall painting of Zapata shows how powerful the people thought this leader was during the Mexican Revolution.

Mexico Today

After the revolution, many Mexican families moved from the countryside to the cities. Others stayed behind to farm the land and sell the crops in local towns and villages.

Ernesto Zedillo Ponce de León is Mexico's current leader until the next election in 2000. He is improving housing, education, and health care for all Mexicans.

Above: After a farmer feeds his family, the rest of the produce is sold at the market.

13

A True Indian Hero

Benito Juárez was **orphaned** at three years of age. He worked in the fields until he was twelve, when he decided to get an education. He graduated from law school and started a career in politics. Juárez became president of Mexico in 1861 and stayed in power for fourteen years. He was the first powerful Indian in independent Mexico and died a national hero.

Below: Mexico was invaded by he French in 1863. Four years later, Juárez and his government overpowered them in battle, and the French left Mexico.

Left: "Pancho" Villa was considered a bandit by many during his lifetime but is now a legendary figure.

The Legend of "Pancho"

Francisco "Pancho" Villa's parents also died when he was very young. He didn't go to school, but he taught himself to read and write. He was a courageous and famous soldier in the revolution. Pancho continued fighting for the rights of the peasants of Mexico after the war. In 1923, he was **assassinated** by outlaws on his ranch.

Government and the Economy

Presidential Power

Mexico is ruled by a president who is voted for in an **election** every six years. Each president of Mexico can hold power for one term of six years. The president's office is in the National Palace in Mexico City, the capital of the country.

Below: The National Palace in Mexico City is in the world's second biggest plaza. The plaza is called the *zócalo* (SO-kah-loh).

Mexican Politics

There are three governmental branches in Mexico — the executive, legislative, and judicial. The government is run by one dominant political party. The president is the head of that party. He appoints qualified citizens to serve as **diplomats**, chief military officers, and judges. The main political party in Mexico today is the Institutional Revolutionary Party, which has won every election since it was formed in 1929.

Above: Every young Mexican man must complete military service.

Farming the Land

Agriculture is a big industry in Mexico. Some families have plots of land where they grow their own food, but there are many large areas of farmland in Mexico still owned by a few rich people. Large farms grow fruit, rice, and cotton, but sugarcane and coffee are the most important crops. Most of the sugarcane stays in Mexico, but much of the coffee is exported to other countries.

Below: Many Mexican children in poor, rural areas work on the family's land.

Drilling for Oil

Mexico has many natural **resources**, such as oil and gas. Most of the oil is produced in the northeastern part of the country. A system of pipelines transports the oil to the rest of Mexico and to the border of the United States. Gold, silver, and copper are also mined in Mexico and exported around the world. Mexico trades with the United States, Canada, Japan, Spain, France, Germany, and Brazil.

Above: Oil was discovered in Mexico in 1974.

People and Lifestyle

Mestizos

After the Spanish occupation, the Spanish and the Indians lived peacefully with one another and began to have children together. Children with one Spanish parent and one Indian parent are called *mestizos* (mess-TEE-zos). Today, they make up the majority of the Mexican population.

Below: These four sisters are mestizos. They have a mixture of Indian and Spanish blood.

Left: Mexican families are very close. They work hard together.

Indians

There are still many small Indian communities in Mexico. These Indians live in villages, where they have their own culture and languages and worship their own gods.

One Big Happy Family

Family life is important in Mexico. Children, parents, and grandparents often live together. The father usually goes out to work, and the mother works at home, looking after the children. During the week, everyone in the family eats lunch together. The special day of the week is Sunday, when friends and family visit around a table or even share a picnic!

Below: Food, conversation, and music are all important parts of Mexican family life.

From the Cradle to the Altar

When a baby is born to a Catholic family in Mexico, the child is baptized by a priest. Years later, at the age of about twelve, children are **confirmed** in the Church.

If they are Catholic, Mexican couples who wish to marry have a traditional church wedding. In rural areas, some girls get married as young as fourteen.

Top: Mexican weddings are festive occasions.

Above: Children traditionally wear white for a confirmation ceremony.

23

Education

School is free in Mexico, and children must attend until at least the sixth grade. At fourteen, they decide whether or not to continue their education at secondary school.

After secondary school, students can continue their education at university. Most of the universities in Mexico are located in the big towns and cities. The first Mexican university was opened in Mexico City in 1551 by the King of Spain.

Below: Children in Mexico must attend classes until age fourteen.

Left: Some children earn extra money for their families as street musicians.

Some Mexican families are poor and cannot afford to buy the books and clothes their children need for school. Others keep their children home to work the land. The Mexican government encourages all of its children to go to school.

Left: *Quetzalcoatl* means "feather-covered snake" in the Indian language of Nahuatl.

Gods and Goddesses

Before the Spanish arrived in Mexico, Indians worshiped many different gods. One of the gods was *Quetzalcoatl* (KAYT-sal-koh-AT-ul), the Aztec god of wind and breath. When Hernán Cortés arrived in Mexico, the Aztecs thought he was Quetzalcoatl because he looked so strange to them. Cortés may have conquered the Aztecs because the Indians were so afraid of him.

The Catholic Church

After Cortés's battle with the Aztecs, missionaries arrived in Mexico from the Catholic Church in Spain to teach the native Indians about Christianity. Catholic churches were built throughout Mexico. Today, over 90 percent of the Mexican population is Roman Catholic.

Above: This image of the Virgin Mary is displayed on an enormous banner outside the Basilica of Guadalupe on her feast day.

The Virgin Mary is very important to Mexican Catholics. They call her the Virgin of Guadalupe. In 1754, the Pope declared December 12 a special feast day in her honor.

Left: Some Catholic churches in Mexico, like this one built in 1690, are filled with elaborate carvings painted in gold.

Language

Spanish

The national language of Mexico is Spanish. It is taught in schools. Television and radio broadcasts nationwide are in Spanish.

Mexican Spanish has three different **dialects**. Each dialect comes from a region — Chilango Spanish from south-central Mexico, Norteño Spanish from northern Mexico, and Yucateco Spanish from Yucatán, the home of the Mayan civilization. The Spanish language spoken in Yucatán contains some Mayan words.

Above: This billboard is written in Spanish and English to aid foreign tourists.

Left: Most Mexican newspapers are printed in Spanish.

Indian Languages

Spanish is not the only language spoken in Mexico. The word *Mexico* comes from the Aztec language, Nahuatl. Many Spanish words spoken today, such as *tortilla* (tor-TEE-yaa), and *tamale* (tah-MAH-lay) are **derived** from Nahuatl. There are about fifty Indian languages still spoken in Mexico by a small number of native Indians.

Above: Even if two people speak different Spanish dialects, they will be able to understand one another.

Arts

Before the Spanish invasion of Mexico, native Indian civilizations produced many styles of art. They created sculptures of gods, bright wall paintings called murals, and masks made of gold and silver decorated with colorful stones.

The Indians built huge pyramid-shaped temples in stone, but most of them were destroyed by the Spanish.

Below: This pyramid-shaped temple was built by the Indians in a city called Teotihuacan before the arrival of the Spanish.

A New Style

After the arrival of the Spanish, a new style of architecture appeared in Mexico. *Churrigueresque* (choo-REE-ger-ESK) featured elaborate carvings in stone.

In the twentieth century, Spanish and Indian art styles were combined depicting the European and Indian heritage of the Mexican people.

Above: Huge Churrigueresque carvings of saints and elaborate columns decorate the front of this cathedral in Zacatecas.

31

Music

No celebration takes place in Mexico without music. The most popular style is *norteña* (nor-TAYN-ya), a mixture of sounds from Europe and Mexico. *Tejano* (teh-HAHN-oh) is a combination of Mexican and American music. **Mariachi** (mah-ree-AH-chee) bands take their name from the word *marriage* because they used to perform at weddings. Today, they are popular at many occasions.

Below: There are eight musicians in a mariachi band playing guitars, violins, and trumpets.

Dance

Mexicans also love to dance. Each region in the country has its own dances that are energetically performed in brightly colored costumes. The dances usually originate from either Spanish or Indian heritage.

Leisure

Fiestas are very important to the Mexican people. They are usually religious celebrations held near a church. People wear traditional dress and enjoy dancing and feasting. There are so many fiestas in Mexico that probably somewhere in the country, a fiesta is celebrated every day!

Below: Mexican children love to put on their special festival costumes for a fiesta.

Left: Piñatas are often shaped like clowns or animals.

Party Time

One of the longest celebrations in Mexico is called *posada* (po-SAH-da). This is Christmastime, when processions through the streets represent Mary and Joseph's journey to Bethlehem. Children enjoy a treat called ***piñata*** (peen-YAH-tah) — a figure filled with sweets, which they hit with a stick until it bursts open.

Sports

Fútbol (FOOT-bohl) is Mexico's national sport. It is played throughout the country in towns and villages. Children play fútbol from an early age, and schools hold tournaments with one another. Baseball is popular in Mexico, too. Mexican teams compete in an annual event called the Caribbean World Series, which they have won several times.

Below: Mexican children love to play fútbol, or soccer.

Bullfighting

The sport of bullfighting came to Mexico from Spain. The bullfighter, called a matador, has to kill the bull with a sword. First, the bull is weakened with **lances** and sticks by men called *picadors* (pee-KAH-dors). Although many people consider it a cruel, inhumane sport, bullfighting is the most popular spectator event in Mexico.

Above: The matador waves a cape in front of the bull to make it charge at him.

The Day of the Dead

This festival is probably the most important Indian religious festival in Mexico. It is a day to remember loved ones who have passed away. Food is left out for the dead by their families. People believe that the dead eat the spirit of the food. The next day, everyone celebrates with a feast. The celebration of the spirits of the dead began in ninth-century Europe and came to Mexico from Spain.

Above: On the Day of the Dead, some people wear skeleton costumes!

Holy Week

Easter celebrations last for one week in Mexico. This is Holy Week, and it honors the death of Christ on the cross. In many villages, the crucifixion is acted out on Good Friday. On Easter Saturday, an **effigy**, or model, of Judas is burned. Sometimes the model is gigantic in size and wears a mask. On Easter Sunday, Mexicans have special family feasts.

Opposite: Judas betrayed Christ at the Last Supper so he is thought of as evil.

Food

Mexican food is a wonderful mixture of produce from throughout the world. Garlic came from Spain, crusty bread from France, sausages from Germany, and pasta from Italy.

Mexico has introduced much of its own foods to the rest of the world, too. Corn, tomatoes, potatoes, chocolate, vanilla, chilies, and peanuts originated in Mexico.

Below: Tortillas are a staple part of the diet in Mexico and are eaten at most meals.

Mexican Drinks

Corn is even used to make special fruit drinks in Mexico. Tortilla flour is mixed with water and various fruit juices and served over ice as a refreshing thirst quencher.

Mexicans drink a lot of coffee. It is very strong, so they like to drink it with plenty of sugar. Hot chocolate originated in Mexico, and it is a popular breakfast or supper drink.

Above: In city markets, fruit drinks are served from large jars.

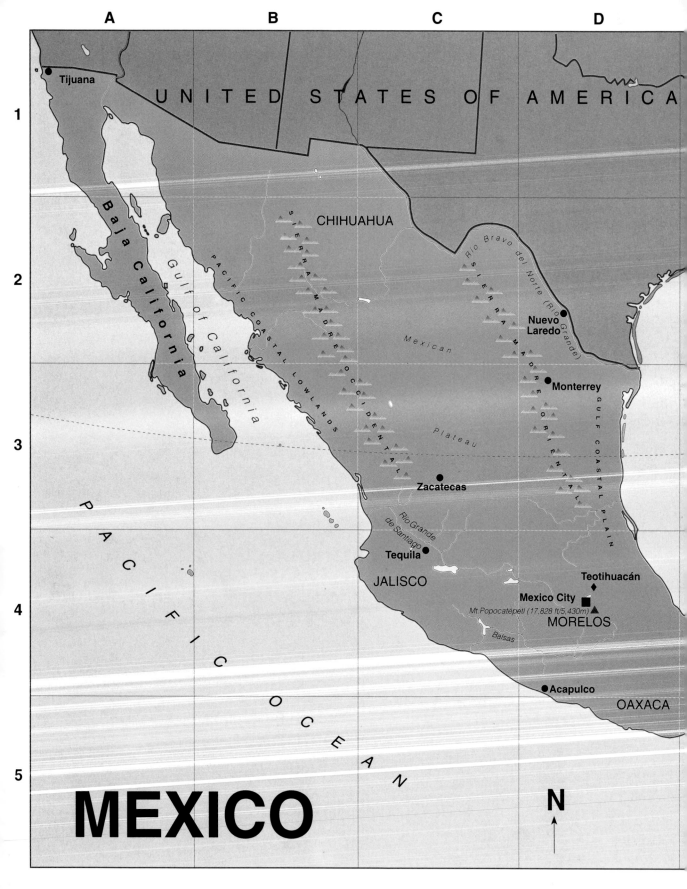

A B C D

UNITED STATES OF AMERICA

1

● Tijuana

Baja California

Gulf of California

PACIFIC COASTAL LOWLANDS

CHIHUAHUA

Rio Bravo del Norte (Rio Grande)

2

SIERRA MADRE OCCIDENTAL

SIERRA MADRE ORIENTAL

Mexican

● Nuevo Laredo

● Monterrey

Plateau

GULF COASTAL PLAIN

3

● Zacatecas

Rio Grande de Santiago

● Tequila

JALISCO

Teotihuacán ♦

Mexico City ■

Mt.Popocatépetl (17,828 ft/5,430m) ▲

MORELOS

Balsas

4

PACIFIC OCEAN

● Acapulco

OAXACA

5

MEXICO

N
↑

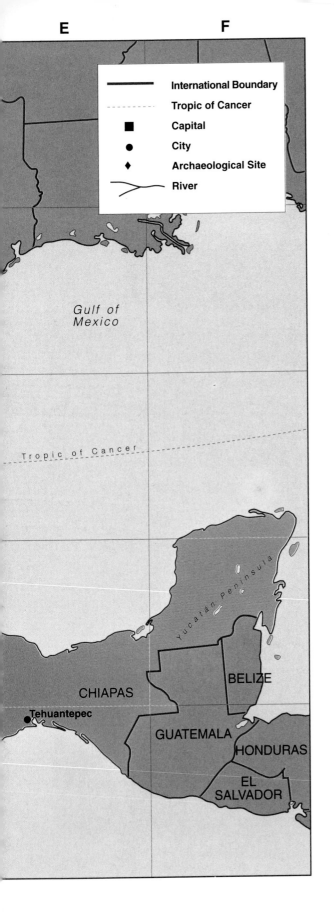

E F

Legend

— International Boundary

---- Tropic of Cancer

■ Capital

● City

♦ Archaeological Site

~~ River

Gulf of Mexico

Tropic of Cancer

Yucatán Peninsula

CHIAPAS

● Tehuantepec

BELIZE

GUATEMALA

HONDURAS

EL SALVADOR

Acapulco D4

Baja California A2–3
Belize F4

Chiapas (state) E4
Chihuahua (state)
    B2–C2

El Salvador F5

Guatemala F5
Gulf of California
    A2-B3
Gulf Coastal Plain
    D3

Gulf of Mexico E2

Honduras F5

Jalisco (state) C4

Mexican Plateau
    C2–C3
Mexico City D4
Monterrey D3
Morelos (state) D4

Nuevo Laredo D2

Oaxaca (state) D5

Pacific Coastal
    Lowlands B2–B3
Pacific Ocean
    A3–C5
Popocatépetl, Mt.
    D4

Río Bravo del Norte
    (Rio Grande)
    C2–D2
Río Grande de
    Santiago C3–C4

Sierra Madre
    Occidental
    B2–C3
Sierra Madre
    Oriental C2–D3

Tehuantepec E5
Teotihuacán D4
Tequila C4
Tijuana A1
Tropic of Cancer E3

United States of
    America A1–F1

Yucatán Peninsula
    F4

Zacatecas C3

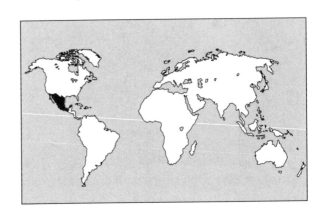

Quick Facts

Official Name	Estado Unidos Mexicanos; United Mexican States
Capital	Mexico City
Official Language	Spanish
Population	92,202,000
Land Area	756,066 square miles/1,958,210 sq. km
States	Aguascalientes, Baja California (Norte and Sur), Campeche, Chiapas, Chihuahua, Coahuila, Colima, Durango, Guanajuato, Guerrero, Hidalgo, Jalisco, Michoacán, Morelos, Nayarit, Nuevo León, Oaxaca, Puebla, Querétaro, Quintana Roo, San Luis Potosí, Sinaloa, Sonora, Tabasco, Tamaulipas, Tlaxcala, Veracruz, Yucatán, Zacatecas
Highest Point	Mount Citlaltepetl (18,855 feet/5,747 m)
Major River	Río Bravo del Norte (Rio Grande)
Main Religion	Roman Catholic
Famous Leaders	Benito Juárez
	Francisco "Pancho" Villa
Currency	Mexican Peso (9.77 pesos = U.S. $1 in 1999)

Opposite: The high cliffs of Acapulco are popular with daring divers.

Glossary

ancestry: family history.

assassinated: murdered for political reasons.

Churrigueresque (choo-REE-ger-ESK): an elaborate architectural style from the eighteenth century.

civil war: a war between two groups of citizens in the same country.

confirmed: made part of a church, such as the Roman Catholic Church.

crest: an emblem or design on a flag or coat of arms.

derived: created from another source.

dialects: forms of a language used in a particular area of a country.

diplomats: government representatives who deal with political problems in other countries.

domination: having authority or power over someone else.

effigy: a model of a real person.

election: the formal vote to elect a government member or party.

hurricanes: violent, destructive tropical wind storms.

lagoons: shallow ponds.

lances: long, sharp-tipped weapons.

mariachi (mah-ree-AH-chee): a type of Mexican music. The band is made up of violins, guitars, and trumpets.

mestizos (mess-TEE-zos): people of mixed Spanish and Indian ancestry.

migrate: to travel from one area to another, usually to escape bad weather or to find food.

orphaned: left alone as a child after the death of parents.

peasants: very poor farm workers.

picadors (pee-KAH-dors): horse riders who stun the bull with a lance in a bullfight.

piñata (peen-YAH-tah): a figure that children break open with a stick to receive the candy inside.

rebellion: a fight against a government or ruler.

resources: natural supplies of materials, such as oil, gas, and coal.

species: a grouping of animals or plants that share similar characteristics.

Tenochtitlan (tay-NOSH-teet-lan): the capital city of the Aztecs, where Mexico City now lies.

More Books to Read

Across the Border. Arleta Richardson (Chariot Family Publishing)

The Ancient Aztecs — Secrets of a Lost Civilization to Unlock and Discover. Fiona MacDonald (Running Press)

Ashes for Gold: A Tale from Mexico. Katherine Maitland (Mondo Publishing)

Aztec, Inca and Maya — Eyewitness Books. Elizabeth Baquedano (Knopf)

Fiesta!: Mexico's Great Celebrations. Elizabeth Silverthorne (Millbrook Press)

The Mexican War of Independence. World History Series. Bruno Leone (Lucerne Books)

Mexico. Festivals of the World series. Elizabeth Berg (Gareth Stevens)

The Mystery of the Ancient Maya. Caroline Meyer (Margaret McElderry)

Videos

500 Nations: Mexico (Warner-Pa)

The Mask of Zorro. (Colombia/Tristar)

Mexico. (Ivn Entertainment)

Mexico: Journey to the Sun. (Ivn Entertainment)

Three Amigos! (HBO Studios)

Web Sites

www.cityview.com/mexico

www.escapeartist.com/mexico

www.mexicoweb.com

www.mexonline.com

Due to the dynamic nature of the Internet, some web sites stay current longer than others. To find additional web sites about Mexico, use a reliable search engine and enter one or more of the following keywords: *Aztecs, Ballet Folklorico, Hernán Cortés, Benito Juárez, Maya, Tenochtitlan, "Pancho Villa," Emiliano Zapata.*

Index

agriculture 18
animals 9, 35
architecture 30, 31
Aztecs 5, 10, 26, 27, 29

baseball 36
bullfighting 37

Catholic 23
chocolate 40, 41
Christmas 35
church 11, 23, 27
civil war 11
climate 8
coatimundi 9
coffee 18, 41
confirmation 23
corn 40, 41
Cortés, Hernán 10, 26, 27

dance 5, 33, 34
Day of the Dead 39
Díaz, Porfirio 12

Easter 39
education 13, 14, 24, 25
election 13, 16, 17
Europe 20, 31, 32, 39, 40
exports 18, 19

families 13, 18, 20, 21, 22, 25, 39
farms 13, 18
Father Hidalgo 11
fiestas 34, 35, 39
flag 5
French 14
fútbol 36

gods 5, 21, 26, 30

independence 11, 14
Indians 5, 10, 14, 20, 21, 26, 29, 30, 31, 33
industry 18

jaguars 9
Juárez, Benito 11, 14

language 21, 26, 28, 29

marriage 23, 32
Maya 5, 28
mestizos 20
Mexican Plateau 7
Mexican Revolution 12, 15
Mexico City 5, 16, 24, 37
Mt. Popocatepetl 6
music 22, 32, 33

Nahuatl 26, 29
National Palace 16
New Spain 10

peasants 12
Ponce de León, Ernesto Zedillo 13

Quetzalcoatl 26

school 14, 24, 25, 28
Sierra Madre Occidental 7
Sierra Madre Oriental 7
Spanish 5, 20, 26, 28, 29, 30, 31, 33
sugarcane 18

Tenochtitlan 10
Teotihuacan 30

United States 6, 19

Villa, Francisco "Pancho" 12, 15
Virgin of Guadalupe 27

whales 9

Zapata, Emiliano 12
zócalo 16

14.85

1/02